Growing up in
INCA TIMES

Brenda Ralph Lewis

Batsford Academic and Educational Limited London

ISBN 0 7134 2736 1

Printed in Hong Kong
for the Publishers Batsford Academic and
Educational Limited
4 Fitzhardinge Street, London W1H 0AH

Frontispiece: **A Peruvian child of today**

Acknowledgment

The Author and Publishers thank the following for their kind permission to reproduce
copyright illustrations: BBC Hulton Picture
Library for figs 4, 5, 11, 30, 39, 45, 47; the
British Library for figs 46, 49; Camera Press
Ltd for figs 7 (Bernard G. Silberstein), 17
(photograph by Alfred Gregory), 19 (photograph by Patrick Knight), 20 (photograph by
Alfred Gregory), 34 (photograph by Suzanne
Hill), 44 (Bernard G. Silberstein); Dover
Publications for fig 48; Pat Hodgson Library
for figs 2, 27, 28, 32; Jaime Leon for figs 6,
13, 15, 38, 51, 52; Mr H.R. Lewis for figs 8,
9, 10: Musée de l'Homme for figs 3, 12, 21,
22, 24, 25, 26, 29, 30, 31, 33, 37, 42, 43.
Thanks also are due to Pat Hodgson for the
picture research on this book.

Contents

The Illustrations

1 Sapa Inca, the Supreme Lord

When Prince Atahualpa was about eleven years old, his father, Huayna Capac, twelfth Sapa Inca (Supreme Lord) of the Empire of Tahuantinsuyu, took him on a war expedition against the tribes living in and around Quito. Quito, now capital of the modern South American state of Ecuador, was the one region nearby which had not been conquered by the Sapa Inca and his mighty army. The year was around 1513 in the European calendar, and twenty years had passed since Huayna Capac, then aged sixteen, had become Supreme Lord of his empire, high up in the Andes Mountains.

The Inca Empire

This empire had been conquered, like the Roman Empire in Europe, by sheer force and superior military skills. Seventy-five years earlier, in about 1438 by European reckoning, the rule of the Incas had extended only over tribes living in and around the valley and town of Cuzco. Now, by a series of successful conquests, the Empire of Tahuantinsuyu, a word which meant "land of the four quarters", stretched over 990,000 square kilometres of the western coast of South America, from Ecuador through present-day Peru and into Chile.

As Huayna Capac was carried in his magnificent litter along the mountain roads and across the rope bridges spanning deep ravines, he had no doubt that this latest military venture against Quito would be just as successful as all the previous wars the Incas had fought. No other tribe had

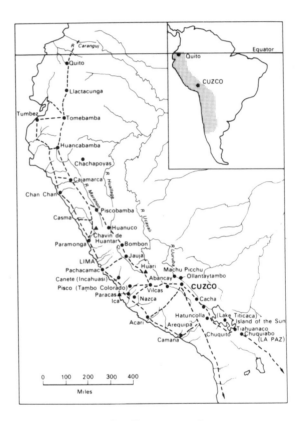

1   The Inca empire. The extent of the empire and the northern half of the Andean area, showing the main roads and towns.

been able to stand against the Inca army since 1437, and on this particular expedition Huayna Capac was accompanied by 300,000 well-disciplined and well-trained men. Long before Huayna had set out, stores had been placed in the "tambos" or depots that lay along the mountain roads. Therefore the Inca army had no need for llamas loaded

5

2 The Incas hung rope bridges across deep ravines. The traveller Squier found that the same type of bridge was still used in Peru in 1877. This is a drawing from his book *Peru*.

with supplies, which would have slowed them down, and they were able to move very swiftly. Often, the Incas attacked their enemies long before they were expected, and their opponents were already shocked, surprised and disorganized even before the battle began.

For good measure, though, Inca warriors would frighten their opponents a little more, by thumping on tambourines, playing harsh, grating music on bone flutes, yelling dreadful insults and boasting loudly of how brave and strong they were. When the battle began, the sling-men peppered the enemy with stones and the archers showered them with hundreds of arrows. Then, the club-men, axe-men and spearmen swarmed down on the enemy, battering about them in savage hand-to-hand fighting until, at last, hundreds of dead lay scattered over the battlefield, and the Sapa Inca had triumphed over yet another mountain tribe.

As Atahualpa travelled with his father along the mountain roads, listening to the regular tramping beat of the soldiers' feet and enjoying the brilliant sunlight as it blazed down from the bright blue mountain sky, he quite probably thought of the grand display of military might which he was going to witness. Afterwards, Atahualpa knew, thousands of captives would be taken to the great Sun Temple in Cuzco, and there they would be made to lie flat on the ground while his father placed his foot on their necks or backs. "On my enemies I step!" Huayna Capac would cry, and the captives would know then that he was their Supreme Lord and master, to be obeyed without question.

Naturally, there would be great celebrations after the victory, with "harevecs", or poets, reciting great epic poems commemorating the event. We would find some of these poems quite grisly. But Atahualpa would not have felt so, since he lived in a society where people thought that war was a natural occupation for human beings, and that conquest and plunder were the right of the best and strongest warriors. Atahualpa was therefore quite accustomed, even while still a young boy, to poems in which triumphant Inca warriors would declare:

We will drink from his skull,
We will adorn ourselves with his teeth,
With his bones we shall make flutes,
And we will dance to the sound of a drum
Made from his skin . . .

This, in fact, was the sort of thing that did occur after a battle, for the Inca nobles used to drink "chicha" beer from cups made from the skulls of their dead enemies. Flutes were fashioned from the thigh bones of the dead, while soldiers' drums were made from the skin of slaughtered prisoners.

Atahualpa might be allowed to drink some "chicha" from a skull-cup and play a drum made from human skin, but at age eleven, he was too young to take part in a battle himself. That would not be possible for another five years, when he would

graduate from one of the military schools which all young Inca nobles attended.

Atahualpa was probably rather impatient for the day when he would be old enough to bear arms and fight for the Sapa Inca. In the meantime, though, he could content himself with the thought that he was highly privileged to be taken on a campaign while still so young, all the more so because he was only one of Huayna Capac's many sons.

Later, when the conquest of Quito and its tribes had been accomplished, as Huayna Capac so confidently expected, Atahualpa would go to live with his father in the magnificent new palace which he had built in his new domain.

All this was rather unusual, a special favour shown by a fond father to a particularly beloved son. Life in the Empire of Tahuantinsuyu was usually conducted in a very rigid way with people living their lives exactly according to the laws and customs. This applied even to royal princes like Atahualpa, for the ideas of personal freedom, choice of work, even freedom of thought, that we take for granted today, hardly ever occurred to the Incas, whether princes or humble farmers.

An inhabitant of Tahuantinsuyu whose father was a farmer also had to become a farmer, and so did his son and his grandson. None of them expected anything in life except to work hard on the terraces cut into the steep mountainsides to produce maize, potatoes, fruits and other foods. Between the ages of twenty-five and fifty, all the men expected to give five years' working time to the government: this was called their "mita" or compulsory service, and it could be performed by serving in the army, or building temples, streets or towns, or working in the gold and silver mines.

No-one seriously questioned whether or not they really wanted to spend their lives in this way. This was the only sort of life they could have, because this was how they

CONQVISTA
LEVÃTOSE·POR·REI·Ī
GA·MANGO   INGA

trono y aciento del ynga llama
do·usno·
enclusio

mangoynga

were born to live. The subjects of the Sapa Inca knew this, as certainly as they knew that the Inca himself was a god, a direct descendant of the Sun, Inti. Inti, shining brilliantly in the sky, represented Viracocha, the creator of the world. When the Incas looked at the Sun, they believed that they were looking at Viracocha, who was the giver of all life and the owner of everything and everyone on Earth. So, everything which lay under the Sun belonged to Inti and therefore to the Sapa Inca. The land was his, the soil was his, the people were

◄ 3   The Sapa Inca enthroned and surrounded by his warriors. This is a pen-and-ink sketch from the illustrated manuscript of Don Felipe Huaman Poma de Ayala, a Peruvian Indian whose aim was to give a short history of Peru. You will find several of his drawings of Inca times in this book. He was working at the beginning of the seventeenth century.

4   The Sapa Inca receives gifts and offerings for the Sun from his people. An engraving of 1723.

his property, the vast wealth of gold, which they called the "sweat of the Sun", belonged to him and so did the silver, which was called "the tears of the Moon".

The people of Tahuantinsuyu believed that they travelled the roads, tilled the land, worshipped at temples, mined gold and silver, indeed performed every task only because the Sapa Inca allowed them to do so. This belief made the Sapa Inca, Lord of the World, Son of the Sun, more powerful than any monarch in Europe had ever dreamed of being.

The Sapa Inca

It followed that the Sapa Inca was regarded with tremendous awe and reverence. He was, in fact, so exalted that no one was thought

9

Plate II p. 56.

EMPERORS of PERU.

MANCO CAPAC,

SINCHI ROCA, II.

FIRST INCA.

See p. 136.

LLOQUE YUPANQUI, III.

MAYTA CAPAC, IV.

CAPAC YUPANQUI, V.

INCA ROCA, VI.

Engraved by I. Swaine

Published March 25th 1827.

10

fit to eat meals with him. The Sapa Inca therefore sat alone, and twice a day, at eight o'clock in the morning and at nightfall, gold and silver dishes were brought to him on a fine cotton cloth or on a mat of woven reeds which was laid on the floor. The dishes contained foods like duck, fish, vegetables and fruit. The Sapa Inca also ate the meat of llamas, the camel-like animal which was so common in the Andes Mountains. A handmaiden held the dish in front of the Sapa Inca while he ate with his fingers. Another handmaiden stood by, holding a lump of rock salt in case the Inca wanted to lick it and so make his meal more spicy.

If any gravy or food fell on the Inca's fine vicuna wool tunic, he immediately changed into another garment. The soiled tunic was burned, for the Sapa Inca never wore the same piece of clothing twice, and if there were any of his hairs on one of them, his servants would eat the hairs so that no one could ever touch any part of his sacred body.

A visitor who arrived to ask a favour from the Inca had to take off his sandals and place a small burden on his back — a stone or a package — to demonstrate how humble and lowly he was compared to his sacred master. A petitioner also had to make "mocha", that is a demonstration of reverence for the Sapa Inca. This meant making a clicking noise with your lips, opening your hands and kissing your fingertips. Often, when the Sapa Inca received visitors, attendants would hold a purple cloth veil in front of him, so that no one could gaze on his face.

In 1532 Pedro Pizarro, a 15-year old page, came to Tahuantinsuyu with the

◄ 5   The first six Sapa Incas of Peru, in an engraving dated 1827. These "Emperors" ruled only in the area around Cuzco, though Inca Roca conquered tribes about 32 kilometres to the south, probably in the fourteenth century.

Spanish conquistadors (conquerors) who were drawn there by tales of the empire's fabulous wealth. Pedro observed these rituals and later wrote about them in his *Discovery and Conquest of the Kingdoms of Peru* (1570/1). He was present one day when a "curaca" (governor) arrived at the Sapa Inca's palace rather later than expected. Pedro wrote:

The Inca gave the Lord of the Huaylas limited time in which to go to his estates and return. He took rather longer, and when he came back, he brought a gift of fruit and arrived in the Inca's presence. The Lord of the Huaylas began to tremble in such a manner before the Inca that he was unable to remain on his feet . . . .

The Sapa Inca who inspired such abject terror in a man as important as a curaca was none other than Atahualpa.

The end of the Inca Empire

The reaction of the Lord of the Huaylas was even more remarkable because, at the time, Atahualpa was a prisoner of the Spaniards. He had been Sapa Inca for only a few weeks when the Spaniards took him hostage to ensure the good behaviour of his subjects and so preserve their own safety. For there were less than two hundred Spaniards, while Atahualpa's subjects numbered about six million.

The Spaniards' leader was Pedro's cousin, Francisco Pizarro, a ruffianly, ruthless treasure hunter, but a man of tremendous courage and enterprise. In order to reach Atahualpa's empire and its legendary riches, Pizarro and his men had had to struggle through the Andes Mountains, barely able to breathe in the thin air and frozen to the bone by the icy winds that howled and whistled about the snow-capped peaks. The journey took three months — from August to November 1532 — before Pizarro arrived to confront Atahualpa at the city of

6 The Andes Mountains, the harsh environment in which the Incas lived. The snow cloaking the mountains is an indication of great altitude.

Cajamarca. It was one of the most fateful meetings in all history. For there followed a terrible tale of violence, bad faith, greed and treachery, culminating in Atahualpa's death and the end of the Empire of Tahuantinsuyu.

The empire afterwards became part of a huge Spanish colony, the Viceroyalty of Peru, and Atahualpa's subjects became slaves and servants to their new Spanish masters.

Fortunately, however, not all the Spaniards were gold-hungry brutes or harsh masters. There were scholars, writers, artists, historians and linguists among them and they set about learning all they could about the mountain realm that had been ruled by the Sapa Incas. These Spaniards spent long hours talking to old men and women with good, clear memories who could tell of past events, of battles, of ceremonies in the Sun temples, of thousands of prisoners taken in battle and paraded in the city squares.

Spanish scholars also explored the capital city of the Incas, Cuzco, and the mighty fortress of Sacsahuaman on the plateau above it. They noted how the Inca builders were able to cut huge blocks of stone, limestone or volcanic rock, that fitted together without the use of mortar. Elsewhere in Tahuantinsuyu they watched fishermen fashioning boats from the totora reeds growing by the shores of Lake Titicaca. And, by riding horses across them at full gallop, the Spaniards tested the phenomenal

7 Cuzco, once the capital city of the Incas, is ➤ today a Spanish-style town. But it still contains reminders of the Incas, as can be seen in picture 9.

8   This rock which the Incas had prepared for splitting can be seen today in Macchu Picchu.

strength of the rope bridges that spanned the deep mountain ravines and gorges.

Above all, those of the Spaniards who sought knowledge as well as, or instead of, gold, saw and wrote about the wealth of the Incas before it was broken up, melted into ingots and transported back to Spain in treasure galleons. From them, we learn of the stupefying riches of the Curi-Cancha, the Golden Enclosure in Cuzco, where there was a fountain covered in gold and etched with an image of the Sun, whole walls plated in gold, and roofs thatched with golden "straw".

The Spaniard, Pedro de Cieza de Leon wrote about the Curi-Cancha:

14

9 An Inca-built street in Cuzco.

[there was a] garden where the clods of earth were pieces of fine gold, and it was artificially sown with cornfields which were of gold, as well as the stems of the leaves and the corncobs. Besides all this, they had more than twenty llamas of gold with their young, and the shepherds, life size, with their slings and crooks to watch them . . . all made of gold.

The Curi-Cancha and its treasures all disappeared. The whole story of Tahuantin-suyu might have vanished too: its everyday life, religion, social structure, agriculture — in fact almost everything about it — because the Incas kept no detailed written records. Only through the observations and writings of Spaniards like Pedro de Cieza de Leon, combined with the more recent work by archaeologists, can we know what it was like to live, work, and grow up in Inca times.

10 Today, on the shores of Lake Titicaca totora reeds are still dried and used to make totora reed boats.

2 The Boyhood of Atahualpa

Atahualpa had his first hair-cut when he was about three years old. It was a very important ceremony, known as "Rutu-Chicoy", and was the occasion for much festivity and merrymaking. For the hair-cutting showed that Atahualpa was now weaned, and was to be set on the path followed by all princes and nobles — the path of careful education, ending in military training and a place in the ruling class of Tahuantinsuyu.

Nearly all members of the ruling class were related to one another, for nearly all were descended from the Sapa Incas

11 The ceremony of Rutu-Chicoy. The Inca baby undergoing this ritual hair-cutting ceremony seems no more pleased about it than some babies at their christenings today. An eighteenth-century engraving

of the past. The Sapa Incas all had many wives, apart from their principal wife, their "coya" (queen), and so they had scores of children. Atahualpa's mother, for instance, was a princess from Quito, and Atahualpa was one of five hundred direct descendants of his father, Huayna Capac.

Therefore, when one of his relatives cut Prince Atahualpa's hair with a knife made from silex (a mineral), hundreds of his royal and noble family were watching. Afterwards, as custom decreed, every member of the royal family was given a small lock of Atahualpa's hair as a keepsake. In return, they gave him presents, usually jewellery or gold or silver, or some splendid woven robe or other garments. The event was marked by a magnificent banquet, with the "harevecs" (poets) reciting verses in praise of the young prince while music was played on reed or terracotta panpipes.

The training of a prince

The training of the royal prince began in earnest almost as soon as the celebrations were over. Atahualpa, like his brothers and half-brothers, was handed over to his teacher, an "amauta". Amautas were the "wise men" of the royal court, whose task it was to teach the princes the history of the Inca tribe. They were also playwrights, whose dramas were acted by the princes and the nobles at court. It is quite possible that Atahualpa took part in some of these plays, which often dealt with historical subjects.

First of all, however, Atahualpa learned Quechua, the official language of Tahuantinsuyu, and was taught all the many rituals and beliefs that made up the religion of the Sun God, Inti. Only nobles and princes received this sort of education, just as only they were taught how to "read" the "quipus" or knotted-string records. One day, it was planned, they would be administrators, or generals in the Inca's army, and therefore they had to know what the records

on the quipus said. Quipus were made up only of knots and twisted fibres interspersed with pieces of coloured wool, but they contained an amazing amount of information. The Quipucamayocas, the keepers of the quipus, could find out from them, for instance, the number of inhabitants in any province of the empire, or the amount of maize in any government storehouse. In addition, the Quipucamayocas acted as "rememberers", who committed to memory, just as a good filing clerk would do, which quipu recorded what piece of information.

Young Prince Atahualpa probably learned how to do quick calculations on the quipus, which worked rather like modern calculators, though of course in very primitive form. Atahualpa learned, too, which coloured wools knotted into a quipu signified such important words as "Inca" or "gold" or "Sun". In fact, Atahualpa could have used the quipus almost as total encyclopaedias for his studies, because they were used to record Inca history too.

The Spanish priest, Antonio Calancha, in 1638 described the circumstances in which quipus were used:

Suppose one wishes to record that in the fourth year of the reign of Manco Capac [the first Sapa Inca], the emperor subdued ten provinces, whose conquest cost him a certain number of men. That in one of them, he took a thousand units of gold and three thousand units of silver, and that in thanksgiving for the victory, he had celebrated a festival in honour of the god, Sun.

All this could be knotted into a quipu and "read" by Quipucamayocas, or by a prince like Atahualpa, "with as much ease as we in our language understood from paper and ink" wrote Pedro de Cieza de Leon.

Atahualpa's studies also included geography, as it was seen from the mountain-

17

CÕTADOR·MAIOR·ITEZORERO
TAVANTIN·SVIO·QVIPOC
CVRACA·CON DOR·CHAVA

con tador ytesorero   con tador

studded world of Tahuantinsuyu. In addition, he learned astronomy, for study of the movements of heavenly bodies was necessary to regulate religious life in Tahuantinsuyu. The timing of festivals had to be exact, so that the gods could be given their proper reverence at the proper time.

The Incas and astronomy

It was necessary, for instance, to be able to predict when solstices and equinoxes would occur during the year, and this was something in which Atahualpa would have taken especial interest. For the place where these important calculations were made was Quito, where his mother was born, and where he lived with his father, Huayna Capac, until Huayna's death in 1527. Quito lies on the equator, where the Sun is directly overhead at noon. According to the Incas, when no shadows were thrown by certain columns at Quito, the god "sat with all his light upon the column".

From the calculations taken at Quito, Inca astronomers were able to reckon the start of the winter solstice in June, which was also the start of the Inca year. This year consisted of twelve months of thirty days each, and observations of the Sun therefore had to be made to make adjustments so that the calendar year of the Incas matched the longer solar year of 365 days.

Atahualpa doubtless learned how to make these observations in one of the solar observatories that were built in Inca cities. Here, some scholars and archaeologists believe, Inca astronomers used the Intihuatana (a stone shaped like an anvil on which the Sun shone directly at certain times) to study the movements of the Sun, the Moon and the planets such as Jupiter, Mars or Mercury. One of the few surviving Intihuatana, a stone prism in the fortress of Macchu Picchu, 122 kilometres northwest of Cuzco, has angles which point to the four compass directions. At about six o'clock in the morning in summer, the rays of the Sun rising over the surrounding mountains strike directly on the stone. In Atahualpa's time, Macchu Picchu, one of a ring of fortresses built to protect Cuzco, was a fairly new city, only about one hundred years old, and it may be that the prince watched this magnificent scene of the Sun on the stone at the very spot which is today the greatest tourist attraction in the whole of South America.

The training of a warrior

The secrets of astronomy were revealed only to nobles of royal blood, like Atahualpa, and the reason was simple. Everyone in Tahuantinsuyu was brought up to "know their place". It was the place, or purpose, of royal princes and nobles to be leaders, and so only they were taught the knowledge of astronomy required to carry out religious ceremonies. Likewise, only Inca nobles attended the military schools, where they learned not simply the art of fighting, but also military tactics and how to direct and control large forces of men — the knowledge they would need as generals in the Inca army. Above all, princes and nobles like Atahualpa had to be especially tough and fearless, and a great deal of training at the military schools was concerned with teaching them how to control natural fear or nervousness when facing situations of danger.

First, though, Inca nobles learned how to use weapons. By European standards, Inca weapons were crude, almost primitive, but they were quite effective. One weapon consisted of three stones tied to the ends of cords: this could be thrown at an enemy's legs, effectively tying them together, and so making him fall to the ground. Another

19

chinchaysuyo

simple, but deadly Inca weapon was a stone- or metal-headed club with six sharp spikes sticking out of it. There were also the more usual bows and arrows, battle-axes fashioned from stone, bronze and copper, double-edged broadswords made from Chonta wood, and spears, 183 centimetres long, made from long shafts of wood with points that had either been hardened in a fire or tipped with metal.

Inca soldiers also had to have protection, and wore a sort of armour made from thick, quilted-cotton tunics, and helmets made of wood or strips of cane. They carried two shields. One, made of strips of palm

◄ **13 The Intihuatana, or "hitching post" of the Sun, at Macchu Picchu. Once there were intihuatana all over Tahuantinsuyu, but the Spaniards destroyed all but a very few of them.**

14 The Incas at war. A general holds his battle standard as soldiers fight the enemy. Chinchaysuyu was one of the four "quarters" of the Inca empire.

and cotton, was worn slung across their backs. The other was made of round or square wooden boards covered in metal or deer-hide. Inca soldiers also protected themselves in battle by wrapping long shawls round parts of the body, round an arm or leg, to shield them from enemy arrows or spears.

Once they knew what weapons could do, students at the military schools were taught how to direct "purics" (warriors) in tactics such as setting fire to grass in order to drive an enemy out into the open. The skill in this was to know exactly when to use the tactic to produce the desired effect.

21

The Incas were also masters of the art of ambush — a natural means of waging war in the sort of country in which they lived. Atahualpa and other young nobles probably marched out to practice-areas in the mountains, where narrow paths led between clumps of rock, or trees growing down a slope offered cover in which to hide and wait for an enemy. Here the nobles practised ambushing each other, and learned to recognize places where enemies might lie in wait to ambush them, so that they could take steps to avoid or get round them.

Graduation day in the military schools arrived when the students were sixteen years old. Already, when they were fourteen, they had gone through their maturity rites (see Chapter 5) and were considered to be fully-grown men. However, before they were regarded as fully-fledged military leaders, they had to undergo severe tests of endurance and courage. The tests lasted one month, and included wrestling, boxing, combat with weapons and running.

Running was particularly important, because the Incas had no horses, and no wheeled vehicles. The animals they did employ, the small llamas, were mainly used as pack animals. So, the fastest-moving creature in Tahuantinsuyu was a human runner, and if he was also a soldier, he had to know how to cover difficult country at the greatest possible speed. This was why the graduation tests included running over a distance of sixteen kilometres across rocks, streams, sheer mountain slopes and thick forests and bush country.

This was not the only form of hardship which the nobles had to endure during their month-long test. They also had to fast, that is, go without food for long periods of time, and they lived only on water and herbs for six days at a stretch. At night they slept on the ground, just as they would have to do one day when out on a military campaign. They wore no sandals, even during the running tests, and dressed in plain garments, often with no extra shawls or coverings to protect them against the sharp cold of the mountain night.

At night the young nobles did sentry duty. This could be an eerie, frightening experience for them, with the great black hulks of the mountains rising on all sides and the calls of night birds echoing between the rock faces. Another test to teach them to conquer fear was to make them stand without flinching while a lance was whipped back and forth only a few centimetres from their faces. From time to time, the nobles were given painful beatings with canes, in order to see how well they could endure pain. In order to pass the test, the nobles had not to wince, cry out or utter any sound while they were beaten.

The young men become warriors

At the end of the month, those who had passed this difficult and frightening test certainly deserved to be deemed "children of the Sun". This was what the Sapa Inca named them, when he presented them with the mark of their success. The Sapa Inca pierced their ears with a golden needle, and the holes were kept open, so that later on long pendants or ear-rings could be hung there. These were the symbol of the Inca nobility and were so heavy that they could stretch the ear-lobes down to the shoulders. This was why the Spaniards nicknamed the Inca nobles "orejones", or "big-ears".

When their ears had been pierced, the young nobles kissed the Inca's hand. Then, they put on special golden sandals. The Sapa Inca kissed each of them on their shoulders. After this, the nobles each received a sash to show that they had now attained full military capabilities. They were garlanded with red and yellow flowers, and their hair was decorated with green leaves.

Atahualpa was given special head-gear, showing that he was of royal blood. This was a yellow fringe of wool with tassels, which he wore round his forehead. Atahualpa also received a special battle-axe and also the sacred black-and-white feathers of the "corequenque" bird. At the end of this ceremony, there was, as we might expect, a great celebration with much singing and dancing and recital of music and poetry.

Before long, the newly graduated nobles were sent to war with one of the Sapa Inca's generals. Atahualpa, once more specially marked out as a royal prince, was given the task of carrying the banner of the rainbow, the mark of his royal Inca family.

15 Llamas. These sturdy, calm-natured animals still provide transport in present-day Peru, just as they did in Inca times.

3 Life in Tahuantinsuyu

Except for royal princes like Atahualpa, or for the nobles, there was no such thing as "childhood" in Tahuantinsuyu — at least not as we understand it. Princes and nobles had to be given a special education for their future positions as administrators, generals and leaders of the empire; these tasks were complicated and required a great deal of special knowledge. However, the rest of the Sapa Inca's subjects, the members of the large family groups known as "ayllus", needed no "formal" education. One of the early Sapa Incas set down the reasons why:

It is not right that the children of plebeians [working people] should be taught knowledge that is only suitable for nobles, lest the lower classes rise up and grow arrogant and bring down the government. It is enough that they learn the trades of their fathers, for governing is no matter for them, and it is discreditable to power and to the state that these should be entrusted to the common people.

Learning the trades of their fathers meant copying what their fathers did: this was the only "education" that ordinary boys and girls had. They learned how to grow and tend crops, how to look after herds of llamas, alpacas or vicunas, and how to weave cloth on looms from the wool of these animals, or from cotton brought in from the upper Amazon River. Youngsters copying their fathers and mothers learned also how to make their own bowls and dishes from clay or wood, and how to trade in the markets, using cloth, pottery, carvings, potatoes, corn and other goods as "money".

The first years of childhood
The only time in their lives that children were not regarded simply as "small adults" was in their first two or three years, when they had no names but were known simply as "wawa" or "baby".

When a baby was born, it was washed in the nearest stream, and when it was four days old it was placed in a cradle known as a "quirau". The mother would carry the baby on her back while she was labouring in the fields or in the house, and if she put the quirau down to do her work, she always kept the baby within easy reach.

◄ 16 An Inca baby in his quirau or cradle.

24

17 Inca babies have been carried on their mothers' backs for centuries. This Peruvian mother follows the tradition today.

Mothers used to breast-feed their babies until they were two years old, but they deliberately refrained from pampering them or even showing them affection because it was thought that this might spoil the children. "The mothers never took the babies into their arms or on their laps. They said it made them cry-babies", wrote Garcilaso de la Vega, who was born in 1601, the son of a Spaniard and an Inca princess. Garcilaso was himself brought up like this, and in his *Royal Commentaries of the Incas* he went on to describe how children old enough to crawl were put into a sort of playpen. This playpen was a hole dug in the ground which came up to the child's armpits. A few small toys were put into the hole for the child to amuse himself with.

Children were not encouraged to play with toys, or at least they were not encouraged to indulge in what was called "unproductive play". They did play at "pisqoynyo" (whipping tops), or games in which counters were thrown. But once they had been weaned, at the age of two or three, and the hair-cutting ceremony of "rutu-chicoy" had been performed, they were expected to begin their working lives.

All this might sound dismal, but it was quite reasonable in the circumstances. In Tahuantinsuyu life was hard, work was hard, and the land and surroundings in which people lived were hard. It followed that the people had to be tough, well-disciplined and not inclined to indulge themselves. Otherwise, they would not have been able to make a proper contribution to the life of their "ayllu".

Children also had to learn strict lessons about how people should behave themselves.

25

By spending their time constantly with their parents and their elders, children soon learned the basic idea behind life in the ayllu. It was "Ama sua, ama llulla, ama cheklla", which meant "Do not steal, do not lie, do not be lazy". Strict rules like this produced a society in which people were remarkably honest and hard-working.

Stealing in Tahuantinsuyu was not only a punishable crime: it was also sacrilege (lack of reverence for the gods), because everything belonged to Inti, the Sun, and so to steal was to steal from the god. Telling a lie was concealing the truth from the god. And to be idle was to disobey the sacred Inca and that was another form of sacrilege.

But, in return for following the rules, the people received real benefits from the Sapa Inca and therefore from the Sun God. Tahuantinsuyu was a sort of "mutual aid" society. While the people did their work and performed their duties, the Sapa Inca and his nobles, who were so grand and magnificent by comparison, also had their duties to observe.

The basic duty of the Sapa Inca was to make sure that his subjects received everything they needed to live properly. In practice, this meant that the Sapa Inca shared out the most important things in the empire he owned — the land for agriculture, the gold, silver and other mines, and the herds of llamas and other animals, which acted as beasts of burden, gave meat and wool for clothes and were used as sacrifices at religious festivals.

Inca farming

The whole land was divided into three. All the food and plants grown on one part went to the gods and their priests. The produce of the second section of land was for the government; from this, the Inca nobles were supplied with food, and so were government officials, craftsmen and the army. Everything grown on the third part of the land went to supply the ordinary people. The boundaries between the three different types of land were carefully and clearly marked. Anyone who dared to move the markers was very severely punished. So was anyone who failed to work the different fields in the proper order. The first and most important was the land set aside for the gods, then came the government's land, then the people's.

Each family received a certain amount of the "people's land" according to how many family members there were. A man and his wife got one "topo" of land, which measured about four thousand square metres. Each of their sons received an extra strip of land and each daughter half a strip.

This share-out of land took place every autumn, that is, in the month of March or April (as Tahuantinsuyu was south of the equator). The people worked to provide the government with maize, quinoa herbs,

◀ **18** The pisqoynyo (top) was spun by whipping it with a lash.

charqui (dried llama meat), as well as cord, hemp, wool, sandals and weapons. These were stored in large baskets, in the government granaries or warehouses.

In August ploughing began, but before this there was a festival. These festivals were so important that the nobility and sometimes the Sapa Inca himself used to attend them. The Spanish historian and Jesuit priest Bernabe Cobo wrote:

If the Inca himself or his governor or some high official happened to be present, he started the work with a golden digging

19   Macchu Picchu. The land was terraced for cultivation.

stick . . . and following his example, all the other officials and nobles who accompanied him did the same.

Then, the men got to work with the "taclla" (foot-plough), a shaft of wood, 183 centimetres long, hardened at the point by fire, or tipped with bronze. As the men turned the earth with the taclla, the women broke up the clods they had cut with a kind of hoe called a "lampa". In September,

27

"sara" (corn) was planted, and in October or November, when the rains began, the potatoes.

The rainy season was supposed to last until May, but the weather varied from year to year, and if the rains did not begin on time, then there was a danger that the crops would fail. A drought was a great disaster and was thought to mean that the gods were not pleased. When this seemed to threaten, the help of the priests was therefore needed. These priests sacrificed llamas to the rain gods, and if that did not work they believed human sacrifices were necessary. They would sacrifice a man, then a woman, and if the rain clouds still refused "to be seeded", the priests sacrificed a child.

A drought in one area was regarded as a calamity for the whole nation. In Cuzco, the Inca capital, men and women dressed in the clothes of mourning, and black llamas were tied up and kept without food or drink. The unfortunate animals became very hungry and started to wail and cry. This, in fact, was just what the Incas wanted, because they believed that the gods could not stand the noise of wailing llamas and, in order to stop it, would make it rain.

However, if all these efforts failed and there was a bad harvest, then the government gave out food and grain from its storehouses to everyone who needed it.

20　Inca governments stored grain in this now ruined rectangular granary. The Inca aqueduct winding through the plains to the right once brought water to the terrace-fields from high up in the Andes Mountains.

21　Storing potatoes. ➤

TRAVAXA
ZARAPAPAAPAICVIAIMO

ray julio chacra conacuy quilla

colcacamayoc
suyenueuo

julio — chacra conacuy

22 Sowing the maize in August. Inca farmers were careful to observe the proper rituals to ensure a good, healthy crop.

They also handed out food freely when there was an earthquake or a storm, and also to people who were blind or crippled and could not do their full share of work on the land. And when there was an especially good harvest, the extra food was shared out equally among the people. We see from this that while Inca society was harsh in many ways, it also had a highly developed system for seeing to its people's welfare.

Lack of rain at planting time was not the only danger to the harvest. When the corn ripened, the harvest could be snatched away by hordes of mountain birds and animals swarming down to feed on it. To prevent this, boys used to disguise themselves in wolves' skins and lie in wait for the birds. As soon as the birds arrived, the boys peppered them with stones from their slings.

23 Incas at work in the fields, harvesting maize in May (left) and digging up potatoes in June (right).

30

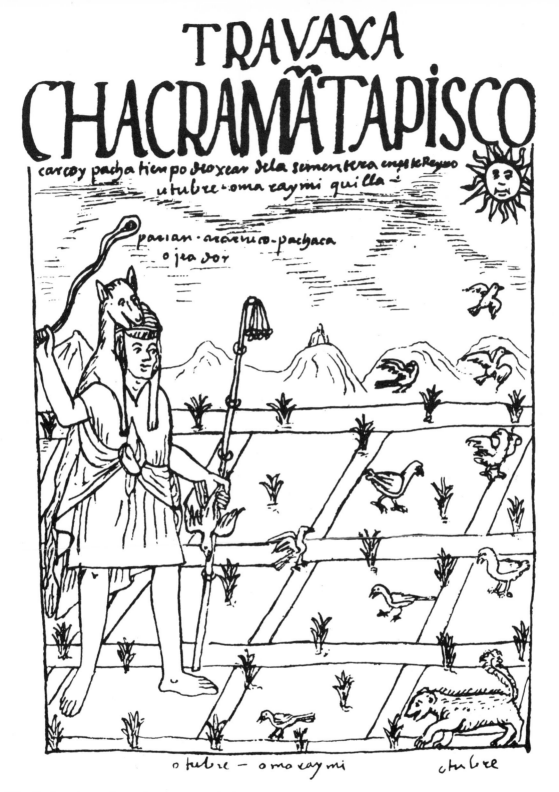

TRAVAXA
CHACRAMÃTAPISCO

carcoy pacha tiempo d~o xcar dela sementera enptkReyno
utubce·oma raymi quilla ·

parian·aracuco·pachaca
o jca dor

otubce — omocaymi   ctubce

24   An Inca boy acts as a human scarecrow.

PRIMERA CALLE
AVACOCVARMI

de edad de treynta y tres años

muger de tributo

When, at long last, the harvest was gathered in, there was a great festival of thanksgiving. The first grains of corn were offered to the gods on family shrines which were set up in the fields. On top of the shrine, which was in the form of a stepped pyramid, there was a wooden or stone image of the local god. These shrines could be very large: some, situated near Lima, the present-day capital of Peru, were made up of more than twelve million bricks.

The mountainous land of Tahuantinsuyu had to be terraced for cultivation (see picture 19). Fields on the sides of hills and mountains were cut into steps and irrigated

ABRIL
CAMAI·IИCAPAIM

fiesta del ynga

ynca

by means of stone-lined channels. The water started off at the top and flowed down each terraced step in a constant stream. The irrigation systems constructed by Inca engineers were very sophisticated, and it was possible to guide water to the fields from as far away as 904 kilometres, where streams poured out of the glaciers thousands of metres up in the snow-capped mountain ranges. The engineers also constructed water reservoirs, like the one running underground at the fortress of Sacsahuaman, in the heights above Cuzco.

Clothes and food

The water needed for irrigation, like the land, was divided up according to the needs of various farmers. Herds of llamas, alpacas and vicunas were also shared out in much the same way. The shares were not strictly equal, because people's needs varied. An ordinary farmer might get only ten llamas. The nobles were allowed a few more, and the largest number belonged to the government. This was because the government needed llamas for many different purposes: they had to provide transport and pack-animals for government officials travelling on official business, and they also had to provide the people with llama and alpaca wool for clothes. Each family received as much wool as it needed for its members, and this was taken home and woven into cloth on simple hand-looms.

Clothes were extremely plain. Everyone wore cotton and llama wool tunics consisting of two rectangles of cloth sewn together, with holes left for the arms and the head. No piece of clothing could be plainer than that, and people were not encouraged to make grander garments for themselves. It was thought that, if they were

26 A puric, or able-bodied worker (right), all dressed up in his best festive clothes, with fringes round his knees and ankles. His everyday working clothes were very much plainer.

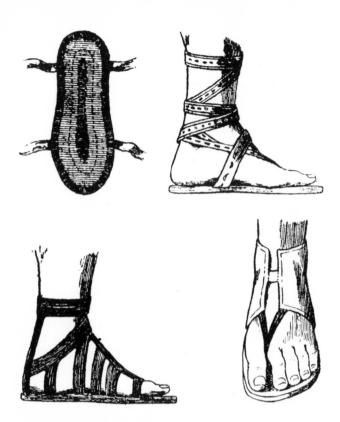

27 Some of the sandals the Incas wore.

interesting patterns, or giving them borders made from squares, diamonds, triangles and other shapes.

Over their tunics, men and women wore cloaks to protect them from the intense cold of this mountain area. Men and women wore identical sandals, which were made from wool, the fibre of aloe plants, or llama hides. The soles of the sandals were often made from the necks of llamas.

The Incas had to be very careful about the number of llamas killed for clothing or for food, since the animals also had such an important part to play in the transport system of Tahuantinsuyu and in Inca religious life. Therefore, although they sometimes ate llama meat, they preferred to get meat from guinea pigs. Apart from this, people lived mainly on a vegetarian diet. Meals usually consisted of boiled or roasted maize, potatoes or a grain called quinea. Sometimes a little meat or herbs such as hot chilis were added to give dishes some extra zest. Fish, various soups and stews, maize cakes made from rough bran, and several different fruits and vegetables were also eaten. These included avocado, manioc, tomatoes, beans, peanuts, bananas, guavas and juices and jams made from red-molle fruit. A particularly delicious treat was popcorn — split, roasted maize — which was cooked on clay stoves fuelled by sticks of burning wood.

too splendidly dressed, they might start getting ideas above their station. But, in spite of government restrictions about their dress, the people sometimes made their tunics look slightly special by dyeing them in brilliant colours, weaving them in

4 The Chosen Women and the Chasquis

Society in Tahuantinsuyu virtually "locked" the great majority of men and women into the place in life into which they had been born. This applied just as much to princes and nobles as it did to ordinary people. Even the "divine" Sapa Inca was supposed to act as his subjects would expect of him, according to tradition.

But there were exceptions to this rule of conformity. People with very special talents might be allowed to "escape" from their

28 The Incas melted down the gold and silver from the mines to make goblets, dishes, jewellery, wall plaques or the fabulous statues and golden garden of the Curi-Cancha.

29 The Sapa Inca and his coya (queen) travelling in their litter.

LAONZENACOIA
RAVAOCLLO

Reyno quito cayanbi guancabilca canori chachapoya

raua

30 Inca ladies at their toilet.

TER3ERAE DAD DE INS PVRVNRVNA

31 It was the task of Inca women to do the work of spinning and weaving cloth. Here the woman on the left is using a distaff to spin thread.

allotted place in life, in order to put those talents to use to the advantage of the Inca state. So, both the individual and the state benefitted. If the Inca goldsmiths had not been freed from their allotted places in life, their talents could not have been used to create the magnificent Curi-Cancha in Cuzco, with its life-like, life-size sculptures. If a special talent for engineering had not been recognized in some Incas, they would never have been "free" to construct the splendid Inca irrigation systems and fast roads. The state would have lost. In the same way boys were chosen for their amazing

speed and hardiness to become "chasquis" (messengers), and so the Sapa Inca had the fast communications he needed to hold power over his far-flung mountain empire.

The Chosen Women

A great deal of the Sapa Inca's power lay in the impression of magnificence he made on his subjects. The more a ruler is surrounded by splendour and ceremony, the more awe-inspiring and dignified he appears, and the more respect he is likely to win from people in general. This is as much the case today as it was in Tahuantinsuyu four centuries ago and more.

In Inca times much of the splendour of the Sapa Inca's court was created by a selected group of specially beautiful, graceful or skilled girls known as the "Chosen Women". A Chosen Woman might be particularly clever at weaving or cooking, or beautiful and charming enough to be considered suitable as a wife of a high-placed official. Some Chosen Women became wives of the Sapa Inca himself: this, of course, was the greatest of all honours for a woman in Tahuantinsuyu, and one that very few girls born into an ordinary "ayllu" could ever hope to achieve.

Such specially gifted girls were not easy to find and the "curacas" (governors) were always on the look-out for them. During the regular census of the population, which included all girls above the age of ten, the "head counters" might draw the curaca's attention to likely candidates. The Sapa Inca also had a special official called the "Apupanaca" whose task was to tour villages in the provinces to select the "prettiest, of best appearance and disposition" from all the nine- or ten-year old girls who were presented to him. Most girls hoped to be chosen, for this was the only way in which they could escape from the strictly regulated life of toil which was the lot of men and women in the ayllu. But many were not selected, and they were known, rather unkindly, as "left-out girls".

The fortunate ones were put into the care of the "Mamacunas", Chosen Women who would teach the girls some of the basic skills and knowledge they would require in their future lives. These included religious rites, dyeing, spinning and weaving wool and cotton, cooking food and making the finest chicha which was used in making sacrifices to the gods. They had to develop these skills to a far higher standard than that required for normal household chores in the ayllu. After about three years, when the girls were thirteen or fourteen, they were sent to Cuzco by the Apupanaca to attend "Inti Raymi", the Festival of the Sun.

There might be as many as fifteen thousand Chosen Women at one time, and some were instructed for the highest honour — attending on the Sapa Inca himself. These were the Chosen Women who held the gold and silver dishes from which the Sapa Inca ate. Their duties included holding out their hands so that the Inca could spit into their palms if he had to clear his throat.

Other Chosen Women were given jobs in the Sun temples located all over Tahuantinsuyu. They were known as Handmaidens of the Sun, and they spent their entire lives performing their religious duties. Because of the sacred nature of their work, the Handmaidens lived in places high up in the Andes mountains where ordinary people could not see them. One such place was Ollantaytambo, a fortress some thirty-nine kilometres from Cuzco.

They came out of these places to attend the great religious festivals where hundreds of them would dance at one time, all clothed in brilliantly-coloured robes, festooned with flowers and golden ornaments. The Chosen Women also tended shrines, such as the shrine of Mama-Quilla (Mother Moon). Here, the Women guarded the great solid silver disc which represented Mama-Quilla, who was supposed to be the wife of Inti, the Sun.

Chosen Women also had the special task of weaving garments for the Sapa Inca and his coya (queen). These garments, which the Sapa Inca wore only once, were made from the finest alpaca and vicuna wools. Some of them were so beautiful that they have been classed among the great works of art of Tahuantinsuyu. Particularly wonderful were the feather tunics worn by the Inca nobles on great state occasions, and made from hundreds of multi-coloured quills taken from jungle birds.

Even though they destroyed so much of it, the Spaniards were constantly astounded by the splendour of Tahuantinsuyu, and they found this feather-work hard to describe. The Spanish Jesuit writer, Bernabe Cobo, wrote of "the lustre, splendour and sheen of the fabrics", but concluded that they "were of such beauty that it is impossible to make them understood unless by showing them". And just as beautiful and just as amazing to the Spaniards was the gold cloth into which the Chosen Women wove gold rings, tiny golden bells or the extra specks of gold known as "chaquira".

The chasquis

The caracas and other officials who were constantly seeking girls suitable to join the ranks of Chosen Women, also looked for young boys with the qualities necessary to make good "chasquis". Quite apart from the ability to run very fast, a boy had to have a very athletic physique and particularly good lungs to become a member of the courier-relay teams on whom communications in the empire depended.

These "chasquis" carried messages, quipus and other news along the mountain roads, running at full speed at about fifteen kilometres per hour or more. They ran for 3.8 kilometres at a stretch — the distance between one "tampu" or post station and the next — which meant that they had to keep up top speed for as long as fifteen minutes.

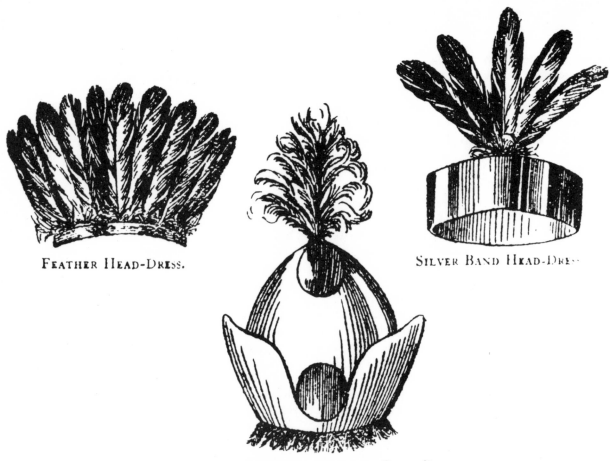

FEATHER HEAD-DRESS.

SILVER BAND HEAD-DRESS

INDIAN HEAD ORNAMENT WITH GOLD PLATES.

32   The feathers of these Inca head-dresses were more valuable to their owners than the silver and gold the Spaniards hungered for.

33   The chasqui (courier) blows a conch-shell to announce his arrival at the tampu station. In his other hand he holds a slingshot and a mace for defence. ▶

On reaching the "tampu" station, the chasqui handed over his message to the next courier, who in his turn ran with it to the next tampu. By this relay system, the chasquis could cover tremendous distances in a very short time. A message could be taken as far as 402 kilometres in a single day and could reach Cuzco from Quito, a distance of 2,012 kilometres, in five days.

Until the coming of motor vehicles, in fact, no-one moved as fast as this anywhere in Europe. Even the couriers of Ancient Rome, who were famous for their speed two thousand years ago, thought that 161 kilometres a day was very good going. But the Inca chasquis moved nearly three times as fast, and not on straight roads like the Roman ones. The roads they sped along were mountain roads, with steps cut in them to allow travellers to get up the steep slopes of the Andes Mountains.

The chasquis' tremendous speeds made it possible for the Sapa Inca to have fresh

CORE ON MAJOR I MENOR
HATVNCHASQVÍCHVRV
MVLLO·CHASQVÍ·CVRACA~

corre on   ha run

34 These alpacas follow an old Inca trail near Cuzco, with the gorge of the Urubamba river below.

fish at meals, even though the nearest source of this food was at least 209 kilometres away — the shortest distance between Cuzco and the Pacific coast. The chasquis were also extremely important as an early warning system, a very necessary thing in an empire which ruled over many conquered territories and tribes. If an uprising or other trouble occurred in some distant part of Tahuantinsuyu, the sooner the news reached the Sapa Inca and his generals, the sooner an army could be sent to deal with it. And the sooner the army dealt with it, the less likely the rebellion was to spread or get out of hand.

The Spaniards were so impressed with the efficiency of the courier system, that chasquis were still being used in the Spanish Viceroyalty of Peru in 1800. Pedro de Cieza de Leon wrote:

The Incas invented a system of posts which was the best that could be thought of or imagined. It may be certain that . . . news could not have been conveyed with greater speed on swift horses.

The most astonishing feature of the Inca "system of posts" was that it operated at heights of up to 5,181 metres above sea level. The lowest level at which the chasquis ran was probably around 1,829 metres above sea level. Even at this height, the air is so thin and has so little oxygen in it that the strain of physical exertion on the human heart and lungs can be almost unbearable. Francisco Pizarro and his Spaniards, on their way to conquer the Inca empire, endured tremendous sufferings when they climbed up into the Andes from the Pacific coast in 1532, because they were quite unused to the conditions they found at such heights. They found that they could not breathe properly, and that they could not move their arms and legs without great effort. They felt sick, suffered from blinding headaches and bouts of dizziness. Many Spaniards died from sheer exhaustion during this terrible journey, while some died from heart attacks.

Although all the inhabitants of Tahuantinsuyu were used to living in the mountains, and were born with the deep chests, large lungs and sturdy legs and feet to cope with it, they did not all live at the same height. In fact, whenever the Inca government decided to transfer people from one district to another — perhaps to settle in a newly conquered region — they always took into account the height to which people were accustomed and which they could stand. People used to living in Cajamarca, 2,743 metres above sea level could, for instance, suffer from "altitude sickness" if they went up to Cuzco, at 3,475 metres, or Lake Titicaca at 3,810 metres above sea level.

The chasquis, however, had to cope with all the heights at which the towns or the tampu stations were placed — and they had to do so while moving at tremendous speeds. It is no wonder, then, that chasquis had to be trained for their work from the time they were young boys. Running, racing and scaling hills was an important part of growing up for them. Their legs had to be particularly strong, and their toes, which were slightly splayed, or spread out, had to be able to grip well on the uneven surfaces they

covered. Quite probably, boys suitable to become chasquis were born with abnormally large lungs. This gave them a good start, for these lungs could be developed by training so that the runners could breathe properly in the thin atmosphere of the Andes and take in the oxygen they needed to keep running.

It was also fearsomely cold in the great heights, even in summer, and thirst and fatigue were other dangers. This was why chasquis were among the few people in the empire who were allowed to chew coca leaves (cocaine), which the Incas called "the divine plant". The nobles and the amautas, the Inca teachers, were probably the only other people allowed to chew coca, which had the effect of making them less vulnerable to cold, hunger, tiredness and thirst.

Once a boy was sufficiently trained and experienced to join the courier-service, he was given a special badge of office. A chasqui worked for fifteen days at a time, and most of this time was spent waiting at the tampu station and watching the road for another chasqui to arrive. An approaching chasqui blew on a conch-shell to announce his arrival. He would also be carrying a mace (spiked iron club) and a sling to defend himself if he should be attacked on the lonely roads. When the incoming chasqui arrived, he had to repeat his message to the next messenger and hand over the quipu on which the message was recorded. There were very severe punishments for chasquis who did not do everything according to the orders they had been given. They could be punished with death if they did not pass on their message correctly or if they gave it to anyone but the next chasqui.

5 Sun Worship in Tahuantinsuyu

To the people of Tahuantinsuyu, it seemed only natural to worship the Sun, and to believe that there were gods who made thunderstorms, earthquakes and rain. It seemed natural too, to believe that spirits living in the earth made the crops grow, or controlled the flow of the streams and rivers. After all, without the Sun the world would die, and without rain the crops would fail. And if a thunderstorm or earthquake occurred, the result could be disaster, destruction and death for thousands of people.

Like all people who depend on agriculture in order to live, the Inca people were always at risk from the fact that nature is unpredictable. This was why it was so important to make regular sacrifices and offer prayers to Illapa, the thunder god, for otherwise he might pour down floods of rain and destroy fields and houses. Similarly, the great god, Viracocha, who had

35 To the Incas the Sun — their god Inti — was the giver of all life. Here, Incas worship an idol of Inti (right) with great fervour.

created the earth, had to be kept in a good mood, or he would make volcanoes erupt and split the earth open, releasing the fire-devils that lay beneath ready to burn everything to ashes in great fires.

The religious festivals

Pleasing the gods was so vital to the Incas and so much part of their everyday life that the year was virtually one long succession of rituals, ceremonies, sacrifices and prayers.

36 During the month of Ayamarca (November) mummies of the dead were taken from their graves and honoured with dances and rituals.

The very names of the months in the Inca calendar were names of religious festivals: Airiway (April) meant Dance of Young Maize; Aimuari (May) meant Song of the Harvest; there was Coya Raymi (September), the Festival of the Queen, and Uma Raymi (October), the Festival of the Water.

In November, called "Ayamarca", or Procession of the Dead, dead people were honoured in a ceremony in which they were taken from their graves and given offerings of gifts and food. It was during Ayamarca that the "Huarachico" rites began. These were the rites which celebrated the beginning of maturity for boys of about fourteen. Huarachico was very long and complicated and went on into December or "Capac Raymi", the month of the Magnificent Festival. This was the time of year when the four provinces of Tahuantinsuyu sent gifts and tributes to the Sapa Inca in Cuzco. The sons of important nobles celebrated their Huarachico here, while sons of lesser nobles held celebrations in their own provincial towns. Maturity ceremonies for ordinary boys were simpler family affairs, held within the ayllu.

The Huarachico in Cuzco was prepared for at great length by the boys' families. Mothers wove special vicuna wool shirts for their sons to wear, and white cloaks with red tasselled cords. The boys themselves made a pilgrimage to Huanacauri, about 6½ kilometres from Cuzco, to make sacrifices at the shrine there. The priests gave the boys slings to use, and spread the blood of a sacrificed llama on their faces. Then, the boys returned to Cuzco, taking with them quantities of "ichu" grass. This grass was later used to make mats on which the boys' parents sat to watch the rituals and games which took place during Huarachico.

All this happened during the month of Ayamarca. On the first day of Capac Raymi, the month we call December, the boys were presented to the Sun god, Inti, in the Temple of the Sun at Cuzco. Then they went again to Huanacauri, this time to sacrifice a sacred white llama. The boys' parents accompanied them and, on the way back to Cuzco, they whipped their sons' legs with slings. This was the parents' way of doing homage and showing respect to the gods. When they arrived back in Cuzco, they made more sacrifices and said more prayers, this time to the ancestors of their families. The Incas believed that when people died they became god-like ghosts called "huacas".

A few days later, there followed the great public celebrations of the Huarachico rites, held in the central square of Cuzco in the presence of the Sapa Inca. Boys and girls who were to take part dressed in special robes kept in the storehouses of the Sun god. These consisted of red and white striped shirts, white cloaks and sandals called "usuta", which the boys' male relatives had specially made for them from ichu grass. First there was a special dance, and then the boys raced each other down a steep slope for a distance of about one thousand metres and reached the bottom of the hill to find their parents cheering them and girls waiting to present them with large tumblers of chicha.

There were many more ceremonies of the same sort, many sacrifices, many dances, and during the final rituals, the boys' legs were again whipped with slings. The Sapa Inca personally presented each boy with his breech-clout (trousers) and the gold ear-plugs which were the signs of his noble rank. Finally, the young nobles bathed in the Calipuquio fountain near Cuzco fortress and afterwards exchanged their ceremonial clothing for the black and yellow robes called "nanaclla".

Now the boys were given the names which they would have for the rest of their lives. These were sometimes the names of their fathers or uncles, or they might be taken from the name of some strong, courageous animal or some quality of character that was specially admired. For instance, boys were called Amaru (Dragon), Poma (Puma), or otherwise Yupanqui (honoured) and Cusi (happy).

Girls, too, received their permanent names on reaching the age of womanly maturity, which was usually between eleven and fourteen. The girls were called by names which suggested womanly virtues or beauty, such as Ocllo, which meant "pure", Coyllur, the name of a star, or sometimes Ima Sumac, which meant "how beautiful".

The girls' equivalent of Huarachico was called Quicochico, but unlike the ceremonies for nobly-born boys, this was a simple family affair. Before the celebrations started, a girl spent three days without food and her mother wove new robes for her. On the fourth day, the girl took a bath, and her hair, which was usually long and black, was ceremonially combed and plaited. Then, she dressed in her new robes and white wool sandals. A feast lasting two days followed, with all the family gathering round and giving the girl gifts. It was after this that the girl received her new permanent name, from her most senior male relative.

At most important Inca ceremonies dressing up in brilliant clothes formed an important part of the festivities. The people believed that it pleased their gods to see them colourfully dressed in fresh new garments, and never more so than in the festival of Inti Raymi, which was the greatest festival of all because it honoured the Sun God. In the third week of June, when the winter solstice occurred and the Sun began to move southwards towards the Equator, thus ending the winter for the Incas, the hills around Cuzco were the scene of great ceremonial and celebration as people prepared to honour the great god of the Sun. This was when men put on their brilliantly coloured and patterned head-dresses and their collars made of brightly coloured feathers, or painted their faces red with cinnabar or purple with achoive or genipa plants. Inti Raymi began at dawn and, while the priests chanted hymns and prayers, young children were led round a huge idol of the Sun god. This consisted of a golden disc, usually in the form of a human face with large rays spread-

37 Celebrating the great sun festival, Inti Raymi, in June.

ing out from it. Then, the children, who were normally aged about ten or twelve, were buried alive together with gold and silver objects, llamas and ground sea-shells. Afterwards, there was a great banquet and people danced and sang in the main square of Cuzco.

Inca sacrifices
Unlike the Aztecs of Mexico, who believed that they had to "nourish" the Sun with daily human sacrifices, the Incas did not kill humans very often for the sake of their religion. Boys under the age of ten were considered suitable for use as sacrifices, but only if they belonged to a family

47

◄ 38 The old Inca feast of Inti Raymi is re-enacted every year in June in the old Inca capital of Cuzco. Atahualpa may have looked like this as he arrived for the feast, which took place at the time of the winter solstice.

with many sons. And human sacrifice was performed only on especially important occasions. One was Inti Raymi, and another was the coronation of a new Sapa Inca, when as many as two hundred children might be killed as sacrifices. They were usually about ten years old and the girls among them would be taken from the Acllahuasi, the houses of the Chosen Women. The children were given a lot of food and encouraged to get drunk on great quantities of chicha. Then they were killed and offered to Inti, to ensure that the Sapa

Inca would enjoy good health, long life and a successful reign. Whenever the Sapa Inca fell ill, or if there was a plague or famine, then a ceremony called Capaccocha took place, in which two babies were sacrificed.

It was much more usual, though, for the Incas to sacrifice llamas, guinea pigs, coca leaves, maize, gold and silver ornaments, small human-shaped wood carvings and sometimes beads, shells and feathers. Sometimes, too, they plucked out a few hairs

39 An eclipse of the Sun was a terrifying experience for the Incas. They feared that a monster was gobbling up the Sun and cried, yelled and made loud noises to drive it away. The dogs being beaten add their howls to the din. An eighteenth-century engraving.

from their eyebrows or eyelashes and sacrificed those to the gods, or, like the Aztecs of Mexico, they pricked their ear-lobes and offered the blood that flowed from them.

Food was another offering made to the gods, and each day at the Curi-Cancha in Cuzco, a wood fire was lit at sunrise and sprinkled with food for the Sun god to eat. Later in the day, priests sacrificed a dark red-coloured llama, which was then burned on a coca wood fire.

Superstition

Superstition played a large part in the religion of Tahuantinsuyu, but this is understandable. Most people — and that included even the most educated nobles or priests — simply did not understand how Nature worked. What caused thunderstorms, or earthquakes? What was the reason for that most terrifying occurrence of all, an eclipse of the Sun or Moon when the sky went dark? No one really knew. When an eclipse occurred, everyone from the Sapa Inca

40 Left: Inti, the Sun god, hovers above as the Sapa Inca consults the high priest. Right: a priest seeks an omen for the future by examining the entrails of a llama.

down to the most humble member of any ayllu believed that the heavenly body moving across the face of the Sun or Moon was, in fact, a monster puma or snake intent on gobbling it up. And so everyone — men, women and children — would turn out and yell, shout, shriek, scream, blow trumpets or conch-shells and make a tremendous noise in every possible way in order to frighten the monster away. Some people would even beat their dogs with sticks and canes so that the poor animals would howl with pain and contribute to the general noise. When, at last, the eclipse was over — and it always ended, of course — everyone sighed with relief and offered up heart-felt prayers thanking the gods for the "rescue" of the sacred Sun or Moon.

Anything unusual occurring in the sky was frightening to the Incas. A shooting star, for instance, was a bad omen, for it was thought to foretell some dreadful disaster. The same meaning was understood if a baby was born with a handicap, or if a mother gave birth to twins. When this happened, religious ceremonies had to be performed to drive away the evil spirits which people thought had been present at the birth. The hooting of an owl was thought to mean that somebody would die, and other bad signs were spiders, snakes or toads in a house. If a fire spluttered and gave off sparks, people thought that the fire-spirit was angry and poured a little chicha on the flames to calm it down.

It is not surprising that, believing in signs and omens, people could be influenced by sorcerers, called "omo", who practised black magic. Generally, they were feared because they claimed to speak directly to the dreaded spirits of the night. The Incas believed that it was possible for murder to be committed by sorcery, and in this case, the sorcerer's entire family could be clubbed to death as a punishment.

However, the Incas believed in "white" magic as well as "black" magic. The curing of diseases in Tahuantinsuyu involved casting spells, making incantations and placating the unseen spirts who, the Incas believed, had caused the affliction. And this meant that sorcerers were often tolerated by people in general.

41 A sorcerer's family accused of murder are clubbed to death.

6 Medicine, Magic and Health

Each year, late in the month of Capac Situwa (General Purification and Sacrifice) — the month we call August — there was a solemn ceremony in Cuzco called Citua. This was the time of year when the first rains fell and therefore the time when people were most likely to fall ill. The purpose of the Citua was to drive disease out of the capital city. One hundred warriors gathered in the centre of Cuzco, a group of them facing each one of the four quarters into which the empire was divided. The High Priest of Inti, the Uillac Uma, appeared on the steps of the Sun Temple and a great roar went up from the waiting crowd: "Away with evil!" they cried. At this cry, the warriors ran out of the central square in the direction of the four corners of the empire, until they reached the city limits. More warriors took over from them there, and so the news that evil was to be cast out was taken by relays to places far away from Cuzco, until at last, a warrior would make the motions of throwing it into a river and it was carried away.

Of course, curing disease in Tahuantinsuyu, or indeed anywhere else, could never be quite as simple as this and the Incas used all sorts of plant cures, magic incantations and other methods to enable them to pass from the state of "on-qoy" (illness) to the state of "kamasqi" (cured). The Incas suffered from illnesses common in cold, wet climates like the one in which they lived — pneumonia, bronchitis and colds, for instance. Many young children died from these illnesses. There were also mountain diseases like "verruga", which was caused by an insect and could be caught in valleys that lay some 1,829 metres above sea level. Another horrible disease was "uta" in which ulcers ate away at the human face. And if anyone moved up into higher altitudes than they were used to, they could suffer from "soroche", or altitude sickness. At great heights, 5,790 metres or more, people could suffer from a form of snow blindness called "surumpi" which made the eyelids swell and could cause permanent blindness if it was not properly treated.

The hampi-camayoc

Whenever somebody became ill, the first thing for him to do was to make sacrifices to the gods, with the help of a priest. If this did not cure him, then the "hampi-camayoc", or remedy-keeper, was called in. The hampi-camayoc was both a sorcerer and a homeopathic doctor, that is, a doctor who cures by using plants of various sorts. The hampi-camayoc would decide what had caused the sickness by making sacrifices and consulting the spirits. Illnesses were sometimes thought to be punishments for wrong-doing. If the hampi-camayoc decided that the patient's failure to observe religious duties was the cause of his illness, then he would place a mixture of ground sea-shells, black maize and white maize in the patient's hand. The patient then had to say certain magic words and blow the powdered mixture towards the place where the offended gods were thought to live. To complete the cure, the patient offered coca to the Sun god,

Reyno hasta quichua aymara

chinbo

42 The Incas believed that people who suffered from epileptic fits were possessed by evil demons.

Inti, and scattered small pieces of gold and silver on the ground as an offering to Viracocha, the god who had created the world.

The hampi-camayoc also massaged the sick person's body to "draw out" the sickness. After some minutes, he would produce a stone, a pebble, a pin, a feather or some other small object which he would declare had caused the illness. This must have been done by some sort of conjuring trick.

After this, the hampi-camayoc prescribed medicine to complete the cure. He had many drug-plants to choose from, some of which are still used today in our own medicines.

53

co quero   q̃ los

43 The Incas used drug-plants in curing disease. Some people became addicted to cocaine from the coca plant.

One was quinine, and another was cocaine, which came from the coca plant. Sayri, or tobacco, was used to clear stuffed-up noses, while the juice of the matec-llu, a water plant, was used as an eye bath. There was also the resin of the mulli-tree which was used to heal cuts and wounds.

Inca cures

If a sick person was strong enough to travel,

he could try to cure himself of his illness by going to any place where two rivers joined. There, he rubbed himself all over with a mixture of maize and water. Anyone who broke a bone in his leg or arm had to go back to the place where the accident had occurred and offer sacrifices to placate the god who lived there. For the Incas believed that the victim had somehow angered the god and so made him send punishment in the form of a broken bone.

This may sound "hocus-pocus" to us, but an important part of such cures was that both the patient *and* the hampi-camayoc genuinely believed that they would work. Like much of modern medicine, these cures were a sort of faith-healing. Sometimes, if the illness or the pain was serious enough, this type of treatment could be taken to extreme lengths. First, a small room would be purified by burning some black maize and some white maize. Then the patient was given a drug such as coca to make him drowsy, or else he was hypnotized. Next, surgeons would open his stomach with knives made from obsidian (a type of rock) and would "remove" animals they claimed to find, like snakes or toads or spiders. If this did not work, it was thought to mean that the patient had offended the gods and spirits terribly. The only thing he could do then was to sacrifice one of his own young children.

So we see that Inca surgery, like their medicine, was all mixed up with magic and placating the gods. All the same, Inca surgeons were extremely skilful and in some ways very advanced. They obviously knew that "disinfecting" was necessary long before doctors in the west, because they would "purify" the room in which this strange operation took place. Inca surgeons also understood the art of "trepanning", or mending fractured skulls, and they were able to perform operations inside the head to help people suffering from epilepsy. The surgeons were able to set broken bones, amputate diseased limbs, and cauterize, or burn out wounds to prevent infection.

Inca baths

The Incas also knew that personal cleanliness and good drainage were essential to the general health of the people. When the Spaniards arrived in 1532, they were surprised to discover that towns and villages in Tahuantinsuyu were far cleaner and therefore healthier than the filthy, disease-ridden cities they had left behind in Europe. Inca architects built drains to carry away sewage and dirt, particularly in places where water might collect and form stagnant pools. In addition, the Inca government encouraged people to wash often, and the Sapa Incas themselves set a good example by taking regular baths. They used to wash themselves in sunken baths made from bricks of interlocking stone set in the ground of their palaces. These baths were filled with hot and cold water through copper pipes or drains made of stone. When the royal baths were built near natural hot springs, then the royal bathwater was taken from that.

There was one of these hot springs near Cajamarca, and it was here, in October and November 1532, that the new Sapa Inca, Atahualpa, was enjoying the warm, relaxing baths while he waited for Francisco Pizarro and his group of Spaniards to arrive. The Spaniards were awaited with some excitement because many Incas believed that a very old prophecy was about to come true: that the bearded creator-god, Viracocha, would one day return by sea with his attendants. Chasquis had brought Atahualpa the news that "strange white men with beards" who rode on "great four legged beasts" and were "masters of lightning" had arrived in ships at Tumbez, 483 kilometres from Cajamarca. What this message really meant was that the Spaniards had arrived with their horses and their guns, neither of which the Incas had ever seen before.

Atahualpa might have been among those who believed that Pizarro was Viracocha, and that his 168 men were Viracocha's attendants. Or perhaps he thought himself so all-powerful, and the Spaniards so few in number, that he could defeat them at any time he liked. Either way, Atahualpa made a dreadful mistake, and ultimately, the most fatal mistake for the Inca empire.

44 Baths where the Incas used to wash, located near Sacsahuaman, the fortress above Cuzco.

7 The End of Tahuantinsuyu

In about the year 1521, when Huayna Capac was still Sapa Inca, the chasquis brought news of the arrival of the white-skinned Spaniards on the Pacific coast of South America. Huayna Capac was extremely alarmed to learn this. He had heard of these Spaniards and of their greed for gold. He knew about the terrible destruction they had caused in Panama, Nicaragua, Honduras and on the Caribbean islands, and how they had been turning the people there into slaves.

Portents of disaster

Huayna Capac was afraid that the same fate would befall Tahuantinsuyu, and his fear turned to terror when omens of some dreadful disaster occurred. Tahuantinsuyu suffered a series of violent earthquakes. Huge tidal waves rose up out of the Pacific and swept away Inca villages and settlements on the coast. One night, the Moon was surrounded by three rings, one of which was the colour of blood. The amautas told the horrified Huayna Capac that the three rings showed the coming of plague, war and the destruction of the empire.

Of these disasters, the plague came first. It took the form of a smallpox epidemic in the empire and one of the thousands of victims was Huayna Capac himself. Atahualpa was with his father when he died at his palace in Quito in 1527, and he immediately took over power in Quito, which Huayna Capac had said would be his to rule. Atahualpa sent chasquis to Cuzco to inform his elder half-brother Huascar of their

father's death, then seized Huayna Capac's treasure and took control of his army.

Huascar was infuriated, for he believed that he ought to become Sapa Inca in place of his father. Yet, Huayna Capac had left him only one fifth of Tahuantinsuyu, while the largest share went to his upstart half-brother Atahualpa. Huascar sent a message to Atahualpa demanding that he come to Cuzco and hand over Quito province. If he did not come, then Huascar threatened war. The second prophecy of the amautas, which had so terrified Huayna Capac, seemed to be coming true.

Atahualpa had no intention of obeying his half-brother, nor did he wait for Huascar to attack. Instead, he gathered his army and marched southwards from Quito towards Cuzco. Soon afterwards, the armies of the rival brothers fought the first of many bloody battles to decide who should inherit the empire.

While this violent civil war was being fought, Francisco Pizarro was in Panama in central America, preparing his expedition into Tahuantinsuyu. On 28 December 1531 Pizarro set sail with three ships, one hundred and eighty-three men and thirty-seven horses, bound for Tumbez, on the north-western coast of the great Inca empire.

By the time the Spaniards landed, the civil war was nearing its end. Some time in September 1532, Atahualpa made his camp at Cajamarca, which lay on a plateau 3,048 metres up in the northern Andes. Huascar

45 Francisco Pizarro. ➤

59

was somewhere nearby, and Atahualpa sent out two of his captains with a force of about five thousand men to hunt him down and capture him. The unfortunate Huascar was marching along a small track accompanied by only seven hundred soldiers when Atahualpa's men saw him and attacked fiercely. Huascar and his few soldiers had no chance and, after a short fight, Huascar was captured and taken to Atahualpa. Huascar was imprisoned, and orders were sent out that all his wives and children should be killed. Atahualpa's great generals, Chalcuchima and Quisquis, occupied Cuzco, and Atahualpa proclaimed himself Sapa Inca. There were great celebrations in Cajamarca on this occasion during which Atahualpa put on the scarlet tassel and the crown which were the insignia of his new position.

Cortes meets the Inca

On 24 September 1532, not long after Atahualpa's final triumph, Francisco Pizarro set out to cross the Andes Mountains to Cajamarca with a small force of one hundred and ten soldiers and sixty-seven horsemen, a much smaller force than Huascar had had with him when he was captured. Seven weeks later, on 15 November, they struggled through the last few exhausting kilometres into Cajamarca. Atahualpa received them graciously, and gave instructions that the Spaniards were to be allowed to stay in three houses which had been set aside for their use.

Pizarro, a cunning soldier, realized that his small band of men were in great danger in this lonely place, surrounded by thousands of Incas. He spent the night telling his captains about the plan of action he had worked out for his meeting with Atahualpa the following day.

Next evening, as had been arranged, Atahualpa was carried into the town square of Cajamarca by eighty of his nobles, all clad in rich blue robes. The royal litter was smothered in the brilliantly-coloured feathers of tropical birds, and Atahualpa himself sat on a golden throne with gold and silver ornaments decorating his black glossy hair. His neck was encircled by a large collar made up of emeralds as large as eggs, and his long robe was made of glittering gold cloth. The procession included men wearing gold and silver head-dresses and about five thousand Inca warriors. Walking in front of them came servants, who swept dust and litter out of their way.

The Spaniards gasped at the sumptuous splendour. As the litter-bearers carrying Atahualpa came to a halt in the centre of the square, Pizarro nodded to his priest, Father Vincente de Valverde. Valverde approached Atahualpa and began to explain the doctrines of Christianity. Valverde ended with the demand that Atahualpa become a Christian, together with his people, and also acknowledge King Charles of Spain as his master.

Atahualpa listened to all this with great contempt. He took the Bible which Valverde offered him and, because he had never seen a book before, had some difficulty in opening it. Atahualpa glanced through the pages and at the symbols which he could not understand, then suddenly threw the book on the ground in disgust. Valverde turned pale with shock at this frightful insult to the Holy Bible. According to the chroniclers who later wrote accounts of these events, he ran across the square to where Pizarro was standing and demanded that he attack the heathen barbarians then and there.

This is what Pizarro had planned all along. He gave the pre-arranged signal to the men standing by a large gun which they had hidden close to the square. With a thundering boom, the gun fired and, as the deafening echo rang round the square, one of Pizarro's men blew a long, loud note on a trumpet.

It was a call to battle, and with yells of

46 The massacre at Cajamarca, drawn by Theodore de Bry.

"Santiago!", their war cry, the Spaniards drew their swords and rushed towards the Incas. The Incas, who were unarmed, were completely helpless as the Spaniards stabbed and slashed at them with their weapons. More Spaniards ran into the square from the surrounding streets to join in the slaughter, and soon, dozens of Incas lay on the ground dead or injured. There was blood everywhere and the air was filled with screams, shouts and yells. The hooves of the Spaniards' horses drummed on the stone-paved ground as they rode in to crush the struggling mass of Incas who were trying to escape from the square. With a sharp, crackling noise, the Spaniards fired their muskets straight into the crowd of Incas who were trying to get out through a narrow gateway. Dozens of Incas were shot, crushed or trampled to death.

The noblemen who carried Atahualpa's litter closed round him, trying to protect him. But they, too, were unarmed and, as the Spaniards pushed through to get at Atahualpa, they cut down the nobles with savage sword and dagger thrusts. Soon, the royal litter was surrounded by a pile of the noblemen's bodies. One Spanish soldier came within a few metres of Atahualpa and was just about to strike him down when Pizarro yelled out: "The Sapa Inca is my own prisoner! I want him alive!"

Pizarro rushed up, grabbed Atahualpa by the hair and pulled him out of the litter. As Atahualpa lay helpless on the ground, his hands were tied up and he was roughly

47   Atahualpa, the last independent Sapa Inca chained in his captivity. From an engraving of 1584.

48 The treasure of the Incas — gold and silver breastplates.

pushed through the crowd and into a nearby house. When night fell over Cajamarca, about six thousand Incas lay dead in and around the square and Atahualpa was Pizarro's prisoner.

Atahualpa's plan

Atahualpa was by no means the ignorant heathen barbarian many of the Spaniards imagined him to be. Within a short while he could understand enough Spanish to realize that his jailors talked about little but gold, silver and jewels. Before long, Atahualpa formed a plan by which he hoped to win back his freedom. He offered Pizarro a stupendous ransom to set him free: one room filled with gold and another room filled with silver. Pizarro could hardly refuse.

The room to be filled with gold was 6.7 metres long and 5 metres wide, and the treasure was to be piled to the height of 2.7 metres up the walls. The silver room was smaller, and Atahualpa offered to fill it twice over. Chasquis sped out all over Tahuantinsuyu with the Sapa Inca's orders, and soon, the people began to gather the gold and silver needed to pay the massive ransom. They stripped temple walls of their gold ornaments, took treasures from rooms of palaces, took all the gold and silver out of shrines and large buildings, collected together a huge heap of gold and silver bowls, urns, goblets, bracelets, ear-rings, plates and other precious objects. All these were taken to Cajamarca, and soon the "gold" and "silver" rooms began to fill up.

When, after several months, the ransom had been collected, it amounted to more than £3 million-worth of gold and about twelve tonnes of silver. Some of the more beautiful objects were put aside to be sent to King Charles in Spain. The rest was melted down and divided out among Pizarro's men. Pizarro, naturally, got the largest share, receiving £600,000-worth of gold and silver. He also took Atahualpa's gold throne, which was worth about £250,000.

Atahualpa now expected Pizarro to free him. However, the Spaniards were afraid to let Atahualpa go. They had seen how obedient his subjects were to him, and what great reverence they still had for him even though he was a prisoner. It would be a simple matter, the Spaniards argued, for Atahualpa to order the people to rise up and kill them all if they freed him. This was when the Spaniards decided that Atahualpa had to die. During his eight months in prison, Atahualpa had given orders that his half-brother Huascar was to be killed, and these orders had been carried out. This gave the Spaniards

63

an excuse to put Atahualpa on trial for murder. The punishment, predictably, was death — and worse still, death by burning, the punishment for heretics, people who refused to believe in the currently-accepted Christian doctrines.

Atahualpa was horrified when he heard the news. He had never dreamed that the Spaniards would break their word and not let him go. He wept bitterly and begged Pizarro to spare his life. He promised Pizarro absolute guarantees of safety for himself and his men, and even offered to double the ransom he had already paid. Atahualpa spoke to Pizarro:

What have I or my children done to merit such a fate, and from your hands, too? For you have had nothing but friendship and kindness from my people. You have had your share of my gold, and received many other benefits at my hands.

Pizarro, though a tough soldier, was not without pity, and his young cousin, Pedro, who was present at the time, later wrote of how the conquistador turned away from the Inca's pleading gaze with tears in his eyes. Pizarro was unable to look at Atahualpa, for he knew it would be too dangerous to spare his life.

On the night of Saturday 29 August 1533, Atahualpa, bound hand and foot, was brought into the square at Cajamarca. There, he was chained to the stake where he was to be burned. Atahualpa dreaded this ghastly punishment, not only for the appalling agony he would suffer, but because he believed that if his body was burned, then his soul would be destroyed. If he became a Christian — as Father Valverde had never ceased to urge during his imprisonment — then he would be garrotted (hung) instead. So, despite the fact that he did not believe in Christianity or any of its precepts, Atahualpa allowed Father Valverde to

baptize him. Afterwards, he was placed in a chair and the garrotte — a noose of rope — was placed around his neck. Atahualpa turned to Pizarro with tears pouring down his cheeks, and begged him to take care of his young children. Pizarro promised to do so.

By now, it was growing dark, and the figure of Atahualpa and the Spaniards surrounding him seemed like dark shadows in the dim light of the guttering torches around the square. As the Spaniards chanted hymns, the executioner gave a quick twist of the rope round Atahualpa's neck. Atahualpa gave one gasp, then slumped forward in the chair, dead.

Afterwards, Atahualpa's body was laid out in the square and left there all night so that his people would know he had been executed. The Incas crept into the square, weeping and wailing, and prostrated themselves on the ground before the body of Atahualpa. Next day, during the funeral service which Pizarro ordered all his men to attend, the dead Inca's wives and sisters set up a great clamour of cries and wails, demanding that he be buried in a tomb that was big enough for all of them too, since they wished to be buried with him.

49 Atahualpa's murder, drawn by Theodore de Bry.

Well might they wail and weep and lament. For the third part of the amautas' prophecy had now come true. Within two years of Atahualpa's death, Tahuantinsuyu was totally conquered by the Spaniards and, though there were revolts and attempts to throw out the invaders, the glories of the Inca empire were gone for ever. The

50 Peruvian women and children of today, with the faces of the Incas of yesterday.

magnificent temples were stripped of their treasures, the shrines were broken up by the Spanish priests, and later, they even destroyed the quipu records because they thought they were the books of the Devil.

The Inca heritage today

Tahuantinsuyu became one of many Spanish colonies in South America, and by 1824, when it broke away from Spain and once more became independent — as the modern state of Peru — it had changed almost completely. Almost, but not quite. Today, Cuzco, the former Inca capital, is a Spanish-style colonial town with wide roads, but here and there, the narrow, straight streets which were built by the Inca architects can still be seen. In the streets of Cuzco, Pisac, Cajamarca and other towns in modern Peru, the people crowding the streets still have that long, hawk-faced look with the slightly hooded eyes which Spanish artists noticed when they drew pictures of the Incas of that far-off time. Out in the countryside, in the long stretches of valley

◄ 51 The Inca's chamber in the fortress of Macchu Picchu.

52 Macchu Picchu, the Inca fortress which the Spaniards never found. The mountain on the right is Macchu Picchu ("Big Peak"). The one on the left is Huayna Picchu ("Little Peak").

and mountains ringed by snow-capped peaks, the land is still cut into terraces, just as it was in Inca times, and the llamas still plod along the hill paths, carrying sacks and packages. Lake Titicaca, where, according to legend, the Incas buried vast quantities of treasure, now stretches between Peru and Bolivia, and on its shores, people still cut, stack and dry the reeds to weave into totora reed boats.

And, deep in the mountains, at Macchu Picchu, which the Spaniards looked for during three hundred years but never found, the rays of the morning Sun still strike down between the peaks to "fasten" on their hitching post, the Intihuatana.

Date List

1100 Approx.	Inca tribe established in the Valley of Cuzco (now in Peru).
1350 Approx.	Incas begin expanding their settlements.
1438	Pachacuti, ninth Sapa Inca comes to throne. Makes war on surrounding tribes.
1471	Pachacuti abdicates. Tupac Inca Yupanqui succeeds him as Sapa Inca. Road building in the Andes Mountains.
1480	Inca armies invade Chile.
1492	Inca conquest of Chile completed.
1493	Huayna Capac succeeds his father Tupac Inca Yupanqui as Sapa Inca.
1502	Huayna's son by a Quito princess — Atahualpa — born.
1513	Vasco Nunez de Balboa discovers the Pacific Ocean near Panama. Incas learn of Spaniards' presence in the Americas.
1521	Conquest of the Aztec Empire of Mexico by Hernan Cortes.
1521	Spanish expedition by sea to coast of Peru. Spaniards learn of "Kingdom of Gold", i.e. the Inca empire.
1527	Francisco Pizarro makes his first visit to western coast of South America.
1527	Huayna Capac dies in Quito.
1527-1532	Civil war between Atahualpa and his half-brother Huascar.
1532 May	Francisco Pizarro brings his expedition to Tumbez, on Peruvian coast.
August	Pizarro and Spaniards set off into the Andes Mountains.
November	Atahualpa meets Pizarro and the Spaniards at Cajamarca. Atahualpa captured by Spaniards.
1533	After paying enormous ransom, Atahualpa is put on trial by the Spaniards and executed (29 August).

Glossary

aclla	specially beautiful or gifted girls selected to be trained as Chosen Women.
acllahuasi	houses where the aclla were taught religion and womanly chores by the mamacunas.
alpaca	a kind of llama with long wool.
amauta	wise man.
Antisuyu	one of the four quarters of the Inca empire (the N.E.).
ayllu	community group descended from a common ancestor.
charqui	meat preserved by the method of cutting it into long strips and drying it in the sun.
chasqui	courier, messenger.
chicha	fermented drink made from maize beer.
Chinchaysuyu	one of the four quarters of the Inca empire (the N.W.).
Chosen Women	(aclla and mamacunas) specially beautiful and gifted women chosen for three purposes: to be the wives of nobles or even of the Sapa Inca; to serve religion; or to train future Chosen Women in the acllahuasi.
coca	a low tropical bush whose leaves are used as a stimulant drug.
Collasuyu	one of the four quarters of the Ince empire (the S.E.).
coya	queen or empress (the wife of the Sapa Inca).
Cuntisuyu	one of the four quarters of the Inca empire (the S.W.).
curaca	governor, in charge of the administration of a local population within the Inca empire.
hampi-camayoc	remedy-keeper, curer of diseases.
harevec	poet.
Huanacauri	mountain shrine about 6½ kilometres from Cuzco.
Huarachico	puberty ceremoney for boys.
Illapa	god of thunder.
Inti	Sun god.
Intihuatana	hitching post of the sun.
lampa	short-handled hoe used for breaking up clods and weeding.
llama	woolly animal of the camel family, used in South America as a beast of burden.
mamacuna	Consecrated Virgin or Chosen Woman.
mita	compulsory government service in the army, the public work force or the mines.
mocha	gesture of reverence to a god or the Sapa Inca, consisting of a low bow from the waist, with arms outstretched above the level of the head, a

	clicking of the lips and kissing of the fingertips.
puma	mountain lion, jaguar.
Quechua	official language of Tahuantinsuyu.
Quicochico	puberty rites for girls.
quipu	knotted-string record.
quipucamayoc	keeper of the quipus.
quirau	cradle.
rutu-chicoy	hair-cutting ceremony.
taclla	foot-plough used for breaking up the ground, digging holes and harvesting potatoes.
tambo	shelter or depot on highway.
tampu	post station used by chasquis.
vicuna	South American animal of camel family, used for wool.
Viracocha	creator of the world.

Books for Further Reading

Collier, John, *Indians of the Americas*, New English Library, 1979

Kendall, Ann, *Everyday Life of the Incas*, Batsford, 1973

Lewis, Brenda Ralph, *Great Civilizations: The Incas*, Ladybird, 1978

Prescott, William H., *The Conquest of Peru*, New English Library, 1979

Roberts, David, *In Search of Lost Worlds: Lost City of the Incas*, Owlet Books, 1977

Tames, Richard, *The Conquest of South America*, Methuen Outlines, 1974

Von Hagen, Victor W., *Realm of the Incas*, New English Library, 1961

Index